CONTENTS

PREFACE

York Notes are designed to give you a broader perspective on works of literature studied at GCSE and equivalent levels. We have carried out extensive research into the needs of the modern literature student prior to publishing this new edition. Our research showed that no existing series fully met students' requirements. Rather than present a single authoritative approach, we have provided alternative viewpoints, empowering students to reach their own interpretations of the text. York Notes provide a close examination of the work and include biographical and historical background, summaries, glossaries, analyses of characters, themes, structure and language, cultural connections and literary terms.

If you look at the Contents page you will see the structure for the series. However, there's no need to read from the beginning to the end as you would with a novel, play, poem or short story. Use the Notes in the way that suits you. Our aim is to help you with your understanding of the work, not to dictate how you should learn.

York Notes are written by English teachers and examiners, with an expert knowledge of the subject. They show you how to succeed in coursework and examination assignments, guiding you through the text and offering practical advice. Questions and comments will extend, test and reinforce your knowledge. Attractive colour design and illustrations improve clarity and understanding, making these Notes easy to use and handy for quick reference.

York Notes are ideal for:

- Essay writing
- Exam preparation
- Class discussion

The author of these Notes is Shay Daly. After leaving school to become a professional actor, Shay studied English and Drama at De La Salle College and Manchester University. He has taught in Manchester for over twenty years, first as Head of Drama and now as Head of English at Barlow High School in Didsbury. He is a Senior Examiner and Moderator for an Examination Board.

The text used in these Notes is the Penguin Twentieth-Century Classics Edition, 1961.

Health Warning: **This study guide will enhance your understanding, but should not replace the reading of the original text and/or study in class.**

Gorseinon College

Learning Resource Centre

Belgrave Road : Gorseinon : Swansea : SA4 6RD Tel: (01792) 890731
This book is **YOUR RESPONSIBILITY** and is due for return/renewal
on or before the last date shown.

CLASS NO. 812.52 MIL   **ACC. NO.**

2 6 JAN 2006

1 6 JUN 2006

0 3 FEB 2012

RETURN OR RENEW - DON'T PAY FINES

Longman   York Press

YORK PRESS
322 Old Brompton Road, London SW5 9JH

ADDISON WESLEY LONGMAN LIMITED
Edinburgh Gate, Harlow,
Essex CM20 2JE, United Kingdom
Associated companies, branches and representatives throughout the world

First published 1997
Second impression 1998
ISBN 0-582-31324-4

Designed by Vicki Pacey, Trojan Horse
Illustrated by Chris Price
Typeset by Pantek Arts, Maidstone, Kent
Phototypeset by Gem Graphics, Trenance, Mawgan Porth, Cornwall
Colour reproduction and film output by Spectrum Colour
Produced by Addison Wesley Longman China Limited, Hong Kong

PART ONE

INTRODUCTION

HOW TO STUDY A PLAY

You have bought this book because you wanted to study a play on your own. This may supplement classwork.

- Drama is a special 'kind' of writing (the technical term is 'genre') because it needs a performance in the theatre to arrive at a full interpretation of its meaning. When reading a play you have to imagine how it should be performed; the words alone will not be sufficient. Think of gestures and movements.

- Drama is always about conflict of some sort (it may be below the surface). Identify the conflicts in the play and you will be close to identifying the large ideas or themes which bind all the parts together.

- Make careful notes on themes, characters, plot and any sub-plots of the play.

- Playwrights find non-realistic ways of allowing an audience to see into the minds and motives of their characters. The 'soliloquy', in which a character speaks directly to the audience, is one such device. Does the play you are studying have any such passages?

- Which characters do you like or dislike in the play? Why? Do your sympathies change as you see more of these characters?

- Think of the playwright writing the play. Why were these particular arrangements of events, these particular sets of characters and these particular speeches chosen?

Studying on your own requires self-discipline and a carefully thought-out work plan in order to be effective. Good luck.

Arthur Miller was born a Jew in New York on 17 October 1915. His ancestors had emigrated to America from Poland two generations before. The family were comfortably prosperous until their manufacturing business failed in the depression years. They then moved to Brooklyn where there were many domestic problems. Arthur Miller himself took a job in a warehouse thus enabling him to save some money towards his university fees.

In 1934 he became a student at Michigan University where he studied Economics and History. Eventually, however, he changed his course to English and began to write plays. A number of his scripts won awards. He graduated in 1938 and immediately became a journalist while at the same time writing plays for radio. Later he worked for two years in the Brooklyn Shipyards. While in the shipyards he met many Italian workers and was often invited to their family reunions and celebrations. He was also aware of the tragedies and problems that surrounded the families. Arthur Miller was later to admit that the seeds of his play *A View from the Bridge* were sown during this time with his Italian friends.

Miller's first success as a playwright.

Arthur Miller began writing *The Man who had all the Luck* in 1941 but when it was performed in 1944 it was a failure. In 1947, however, his play *All my Sons* was a resounding success. In 1949 his play *Death of a Salesman* was awarded the Pulitzer Prize. This has been Arthur Miller's major success as a playwright and one which placed him at the very pinnacle of twentieth century drama. Arthur Miller, who had been heavily influenced by Henrik Ibsen, the Norwegian playwright, wrote a version of Ibsen's *An Enemy of the People* in 1950. In 1953 his next major drama, *The Crucible*, was produced. *The Crucible* was written as a reaction to the fear created by the un-American Activities Committee. All those Americans who were regarded as having communist sympathies were seen as undesirable. Many people in the film and theatre business were accused of having left-wing tendencies and Arthur Miller himself was fined when he was found guilty of being involved in communism. The fine, however, was later quashed by the Supreme Court.

A View from the Bridge was first written as a one-act play in verse in 1955. The play was then produced as a two-act play in 1956. In the same year Arthur Miller divorced Mary Slattery whom he had married in 1940. He married the actress Marilyn Monroe, but that marriage was also destined to end in divorce in 1961. Arthur Miller wrote *After the Fall* in 1964 which was interpreted as a commentary on his marriage to Marilyn Monroe and was produced a short time after Monroe's death. *The Price* was written in 1968 and explored the rivalry between brothers and, as in *All My Sons*, the past in relation to the present. He also wrote *The Archbishop's Calling* in 1977, *The American Clock* in 1980 and *Broken Glass* in 1994.

Themes in Miller's plays

Arthur Miller is now regarded as one of the world's greatest dramatists. In his plays he explores the struggles of the ordinary man against authority and insurmountable odds. His examination of the past and how it can haunt the present and the future is a powerful tool in his armoury when writing about the thin line every person walks through life. While examining and exposing man's weaknesses he also shows an understanding of the deep-lying emotions within every human being.

Exploitation of Italian immigrants

In the 1940s Arthur Miller spent two years working with Italians in the shipyards of Brooklyn and was thus able to study the social background of the lives of the dockworkers in that area. He discovered that the people were very poorly paid and he felt that they were being used by the owners. Many of the workers were illegal immigrants and were being exploited by the very people who helped bring them to America. They looked after the immigrants until such time as they had paid for their services and then they were left to fend for themselves.

During this time Arthur Miller had close associations with the families of the dockworkers. In his autobiography (see Literary Terms) *Time Bends* he narrates that a friend told him about a dream he had about an attraction he felt for his cousin. When Arthur Miller interpreted the dream as an indication that the man might have wanted an incestuous relationship with the girl the man was horrified and refused to accept that there might be any truth in what Arthur Miller was saying.

Note the comparison of workers' conditions in Sicily and Brooklyn.

The playwright observed that the dockers waited every day on the waterfront in the hope that they would get a job. He soon realised that this practice was prevalent in Sicily when he visited the country a few years after his experiences in the docks of Brooklyn. Arthur Miller found the practices unacceptable. He saw them as unfair and humiliating. It gave the bosses far too much control over the men and, because of this, created situations which were open to corruption.

It was during this time that Arthur Miller heard the story of a longshoreman who had betrayed two of his own relatives to the Immigration Authorities because he was not happy about the relationship between one of the immigrants and his niece.

All of this was raw material for the play *A View from the Bridge*. At first Arthur Miller wrote a verse play in the form of a Greek tragedy or melodrama (see Literary Terms) in one act. In 1956 he wrote the full-length prose (see Literary Terms) version that we know today.

THE SETTING

The play is set in Red Hook in Brooklyn. Red Hook is a slum area inhabited by the Carbones and their neighbours. Alfieri, the lawyer, views the drama from Brooklyn Bridge. Most of the action takes place in the Carbone's living room and dining room but some scenes are located in the street outside their house. It is important that we see the Carbones as part of the wider community especially towards the end of the play when their private tragedy becomes part of the public stage.

PART TWO

Summaries

General summary

Act 1

Eddie Carbone lives in Red Hook, a slum, with his wife, Beatrice, and Catherine who is Beatrice's niece. Eddie is worried about Catherine leaving the security of the house. Beatrice awaits the arrival of her cousins, Marco and Rodolpho, who are illegal immigrants from Italy. Eddie tells Beatrice and Catherine that they must never talk about the cousins outside the house.

Notice Eddie's attempt to control Catherine's life.

Marco and Rodolpho arrive to a warm welcome. Soon, however, Eddie shows he is uncomfortable because of the attention Catherine is paying Rodolpho. Beatrice feels that Eddie should not interfere. Catherine and Rodolpho begin to fall in love and Eddie attempts to plant doubts in Catherine's mind about the Italian.

Eddie visits Alfieri but the lawyer tells him that no law has been broken other than the laws regulating immigration.

At home Eddie listens to the Italians telling Catherine and Beatrice about their life at home in Italy. Eddie turns on Rodolpho and accuses him of not behaving according to the American code. He tells Rodolpho that he is not happy about the relationship he has established with Catherine. Rodolpho allows Eddie to show him how to box. Eddie hits him and Marco

Marco establishes control.

intervenes by challenging Eddie to a chair-lifting contest. Marco lifts the chair without effort and holds it above his head while looking directly at Eddie.

Act 2

Eddie enters the house and realises that Catherine and Rodolpho have been making love. He orders Rodolpho out of his house. Immediately Catherine threatens to leave. Eddie kisses her and then insults Rodolpho by kissing him also.

Eddie phones the Immigration Authorities to inform them that Marco and Rodolpho are illegal immigrants. He then returns home where he discovers that Catherine is determined to marry Rodolpho. The Immigration Officers enter and arrest Marco and Rodolpho and also the two other illegal immigrants who have just arrived. Catherine, Beatrice and, finally, Marco realise that Eddie has informed on the brothers. Marco spits at Eddie who threatens to kill him. Eddie protests his innocence.

Alfieri persuades Marco to promise not to attack Eddie. Without this promise he cannot arrange bail for the brothers. Marco will have to return to Italy but Rodolpho's marriage to Catherine will allow the younger cousin to stay in America, legally.

Beatrice is making arrangements to go to Catherine's wedding when Eddie tells her that if she goes she must not return to the house. Rodolpho returns and tries to persuade Eddie to leave because Marco is coming for revenge. Beatrice now confronts Eddie with the truth about his feelings for Catherine but Eddie will not accept her accusations.

Eddie accuses Marco of lying about him. Marco attacks Eddie who pulls out a knife. Marco turns the knife on Eddie and he dies as Catherine and Beatrice attempt to comfort him.

Alfieri concludes the play by telling the audience that it is better to settle for less than the whole truth but that he does admire a man who allows himself to be 'wholly known'.

DETAILED SUMMARIES

ACT I

PART ONE

(pp. 11–33) Alfieri enters and immediately creates the atmosphere (see Literary Terms) – the atmosphere of a place where crime was once set into the very fabric of the neighbourhood. He tells the audience about the importance of justice but, he says, justice is often administered outside rather than inside the law. He mentions Al Capone and Frankie Yale and, later, Caesar himself to emphasise that the present case he is about to handle may not be very different from many of the 'bloody causes' that have occurred throughout the history of Italy. He is also stating that the conflict, like all the others, is beyond the power of everybody to stop it. Most of the time, however, there is a veneer of respectability. Most of the time people are quite civilised.

Consider the way in which Alfieri talks about justice. Look at the way other characters seek justice in other parts of the play.

He introduces Eddie Carbone.

Eddie enters and speaks to Catherine, his niece. At first he is very proud of the way she looks 'like one of them girls that went to college' but he is soon irritated because, he feels, her skirt is too short, and her walk is provocative. Catherine is upset because she is desperate for his approval.

He now informs Beatrice that her cousins have arrived from Italy. This is a tense, exciting moment for Beatrice. She is afraid of the consequences if they are caught but she is very eager to meet the two men. She worries that the house is not as it should be. Eddie takes control and attempts to calm her but then adds to her tension and sense of guilt when he reminds her that she promised to cover the chair. Almost immediately he introduces a sense of perspective when he assures Beatrice that she is saving her cousins' lives. Again, however, Eddie accuses Beatrice that she is always prepared to help her relatives at his expense. But after all this he succeeds in persuading Beatrice that he is a very generous person.

It is obvious that Beatrice and Catherine are nervous before telling Eddie that Catherine wishes to accept the job she has been offered. Immediately Eddie raises objections. He says he wants her to complete her education, he doesn't care for the neighbourhood she would be working in and he doesn't like the sailors and plumbers with whom she would be in contact. He wants her to be able to rise above her present situation – to be in a different class. However Beatrice shows how forceful she can be when she persuades Eddie to allow Catherine to work. Catherine responds very emotionally but Eddie attempts to dampen her spirits when he suggests that not everybody she works with will be trustworthy.

Notice the way Eddie treats Catherine and also the way in which Beatrice reacts to this treatment.

There is some light banter before the atmosphere (see Literary Terms) changes again. Beatrice asks the time and the conversation turns to the cousins' arrival. Catherine worries about hiding the cousins' identity – they might be seen entering and leaving the house. Eddie insists that it does not matter what people think, it is important that Catherine, Beatrice and himself do not talk about the cousins to anybody. Beatrice then narrates the story of Vinny Bolzano who informed the Authorities about an uncle who was staying with the family. When the family discovered that Vinny was the informer they treated him as an outcast and he had to leave the area. Eddie then outlines the way the illegal immigrants are looked after until they have paid their dues to those who shipped them in.

Note the importance of the story about the informer.

There is a quiet moment when Eddie turns to Catherine and says that he never expected her to grow

Part One (pp. 11–33)

up. While she is out of the room Eddie asks Beatrice why she is always angry with him recently. Beatrice denies this and repeats the word 'mad' three times perhaps indicating that she worries about Eddie's sanity. Catherine returns with a cigar and lights it for Eddie.

Alfieri tells the audience that Eddie does what is required and no more. Marco and Rodolpho are escorted to Eddie's house by Tony who makes it quite clear that they are now on their own but they must go to work.

Beatrice, Catherine and Eddie give a warm welcome to the cousins. Marco assures Eddie that they will not outstay their welcome because he realises that the house is small. Catherine notices the fact that there is a marked difference in the colour of the two men. To her *Consider the* annoyance, Eddie interrupts. He tells Marco and *differences between* Rodolpho that they have to work on the piers, work *the characters* they have never undertaken before. The men describe *Marco and* the work in Italy, Marco seriously but Rodolpho *Rodolpho.* laughing all the time. Rodolpho paints a picture of a poor peasant town. Marco, however, talks about his own situation. He has a family and wife to support and they have very little to eat. He will stay, he says, for six years. He is delighted when Eddie tells him how much they will earn and asks Beatrice if they can stay for a few months in her house because that will enable him to send more money back to his family. Catherine asks Rodolpho if he is married. He replies that he is too poor to marry. Unlike Marco, he wants to stay in America and have a powerful motorcycle. Catherine is very impressed when Rodolpho sings one of her favourite songs. Eddie interrupts with the warning that people will become suspicious if they hear singing in the house because there have never been singers there before. He is not happy with the situation that is developing and shows some hostility towards Rodolpho. He indicates to Catherine that she should change her high heels which she does, reluctantly.

Be aware of Eddie's reaction to Rodolpho.

COMMENT

The play opens with Alfieri's thoughtful analysis of the situation in Red Hook. He speaks in an easy conversational style.

Law and justice are important themes that run through the play. Alfieri touches on these themes in his opening speech. The law is looked on with suspicion but justice is very important. Justice, Alfieri says, was often dispensed by breaking the law and he feels that seeking total justice is an uncomfortable way to live. He, himself, is happy to 'settle for half'.

He senses that there is a timeless quality about this story. Perhaps, he thinks, this very struggle for justice was observed by a lawyer two thousand years ago.

The story is told in a series of flashbacks and Alfieri controls the thread.

Study the language used by the three characters.

Eddie, the protagonist (see Literary Terms), is an unsophisticated longshoreman. His language and that of Catherine and Beatrice betray a colloquialism (see Literary Terms) which is powerful but often hides more than it reveals.

Part One (pp. 11–33)

The relationship between Catherine and Eddie appears open and sincere but there is some uneasiness in the air. Catherine desperately craves Eddie's approval and is very upset when he criticises her clothes. The attraction between the two characters (see Literary Terms) is strong and this causes Eddie to feel pleasure and pain when he looks at Catherine and observes her changing appearance. He feels pain because he wonders how the local young men react when they see her.

Consider Catherine's lack of confidence.

Catherine wants support from Beatrice before she will tell Eddie that she has a job. Her unselfishness shines through, however, when she forgets her own news in order to concentrate on Eddie's important announcement – that the cousins have arrived.

Beatrice is excited and anxious. She is delighted that they have arrived but anxious for their safety. Eddie, however, is confident and shows that he is in charge of the situation. Eddie jokes with Beatrice but there is a hint that he is not totally at ease with the situation.

Eddie disapproves of the fact that Catherine wants to work. He feels that she can rise above their neighbourhood and do better for herself. When alone with Eddie Beatrice attempts to persuade him to allow Catherine her freedom. She is angry when he rejects her advice.

For a moment Eddie allows them to be a family. He shows affection for Catherine when he calls her 'Madonna' before giving her permission to go to work. He also makes it clear that he will feel a great sense of loss when she goes.

There is laughter and good humour when Eddie talks about his work.

The imminent arrival of the cousins casts a gloom over the three of them. Eddie insists that they must never admit that they are harbouring illegal immigrants, they must never talk about the situation.

Eddie prompts Beatrice to tell the story of Vinny Bonzalo. All three characters (see Literary Terms) show their revulsion at the betrayal. The irony will not be lost on the audience at the end of the play.

Alfieri points out the fundamental change that occurred in Eddie's life when the cousins arrive.

Marco is serious and obviously the one in charge. He is quiet, sober and very aware of his position. Rodolpho is full of the joys of life. He is enthusiastic about their new opportunities.

Immediately Eddie alienates himself from Rodolpho and talks almost exclusively to Marco. He quite deliberately ends the conversation between Rodolpho and Catherine.

Note Eddie's ability to destroy harmony.

Rodolpho's vibrant good humour and comic turn of phrase is appreciated by Beatrice and by Catherine. Eddie, however, does not find him humorous and he attempts to prevent him establishing a relationship with Catherine who obviously finds Rodolpho attractive. Rodolpho's singing of *Paper Doll* makes Eddie feel very uncomfortable. Indeed the lyrics could be a comment on the way he feels about Catherine. He rudely interrupts the singer by threatening him that people will be suspicious. He continues his belligerent behaviour by insisting that Catherine change her shoes.

In the final moments of this section Eddie is aware that already there is something between Catherine and Rodolpho when the couple share an intimate moment together.

Part One (pp. 11–33)

GLOSSARY

Calabria an area in the South of Italy

Syracuse a town in Sicily

stenographer an employee who takes notes in shorthand

confirmation a sacrament taken by members of the Christian religion

Saint Agnes a Catholic Church

snitched informed to the authorities

syndicate a group who look after the illegal immigrants

piazza an Italian village square

bel canto solo singing

TEST YOURSELF (Act I, Part One)

A Identify the speaker.

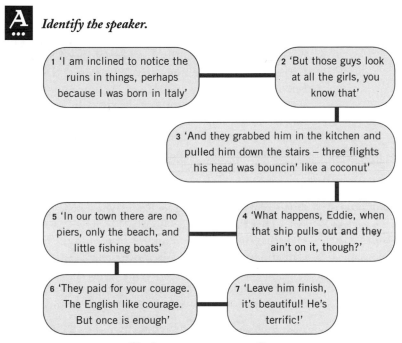

1 'I am inclined to notice the ruins in things, perhaps because I was born in Italy'

2 'But those guys look at all the girls, you know that'

3 'And they grabbed him in the kitchen and pulled him down the stairs – three flights his head was bouncin' like a coconut'

5 'In our town there are no piers, only the beach, and little fishing boats'

4 'What happens, Eddie, when that ship pulls out and they ain't on it, though?'

6 'They paid for your courage. The English like courage. But once is enough'

7 'Leave him finish, it's beautiful! He's terrific!'

Check your answers on page 62.

B Consider these issues.

a The role of Alfieri at the beginning of the play.

b The relationship between Eddie and Catherine during the first section of the play.

c Eddie's attitude to the fact that Catherine wants to take a job.

d The reaction of Catherine, Beatrice and Eddie to the betrayal perpetrated by Vinny Bolzano.

e Catherine's reaction to Rodolpho.

f The contrast shown in the characters (see Literary Terms) of Marco and Rodolpho.

g The contrast in attitudes shown by Eddie and Beatrice to Catherine taking a job.

h Eddie's mood just before Alfieri enters for the second time.

PART TWO

(pp. 33–45)   Alfieri enters and suggests that Eddie's life will never be the same again. His routine has been changed forever. Eddie is on edge when he enters. He is upset that Rodolpho is spending so much of his time on public show. He does not like the fact that Rodolpho is singing on the ships and he feels that the Italian should stay at home when he is not working. He is also unhappy about the amount of time that Catherine is spending with Rodolpho.

Observe the clarity of the comments made by Beatrice. Note her uncompromising stance.   Beatrice makes it clear that she thinks Eddie is jealous of Rodolpho. She then asks Eddie why he has not made love to her for over three months. He, however, refuses to discuss the matter and returns instead to the issue of Catherine and Rodolpho. Beatrice remarks that Eddie's interest is unhealthy. When Eddie meets Mike and Louis they tell him how much they admire Marco for his work rate and how amusing they find Rodolpho.

Catherine and Rodolpho return from the cinema and Eddie shows his disapproval. Rodolpho exits when Eddie indicates that he wishes to speak to Catherine on her own. He tells her how much he misses her and also

y

that he is certain Rodolpho is only going out with her because he wants to become an American citizen when she marries him. Catherine does not believe him but nevertheless Eddie pursues his defamation of the Italian's character. He says that as soon as she marries him he will become an American citizen and then he will divorce her. Catherine is now very upset. Beatrice enters and angrily insists that Eddie leave her alone. Eddie walks off into the house.

Beatrice talks seriously to Catherine about her relationship with Eddie. She says that Eddie will always find something wrong with any boy who is interested in her. She tells Catherine that she must be more independent, more grown-up. She makes it quite clear to Catherine that she is a grown woman and Eddie is a grown man and, because of this, she must behave differently from now on. Catherine assures her that she will but she is afraid because her world is no longer secure.

Look at the 'no-nonsense' approach that Beatrice adopts whenever she is speaking to Catherine.

COMMENT   Alfieri comments on Eddie's troubled future.

Eddie shows his irritation, because Catherine and Rodolpho have not returned from the cinema. Despite Beatrice's effort to calm the situation Eddie will not be persuaded. He regards Rodolpho 'like a weird' and something other than 'a (real) man'. He suggests that the Italian is rather effeminate.

Beatrice is now determined to force Eddie to face some unpleasant facts. She attempts to discuss the flaws in their own relationship but Eddie instead returns to the subject of Rodolpho and Catherine. The tension created between Eddie and Beatrice is too much for Eddie and he walks out.

The undercurrent of the exchange between Eddie and his workmates sets him on edge. This conversation, the

Part Two (pp. 33–45)

Consider Eddie's attempts to destroy Rodolpho in Catherine's mind.

previous accusation by Beatrice and now the excited laughter of Catherine as she returns with Rodolpho are all frustrations that Eddie allows to fuel his inner hostility. He maligns Rodolpho to Catherine when he questions the young man's motives for wanting a relationship with her. Catherine breaks down in the face of his onslaught and attempts to shut him out.

Beatrice, quietly, takes control. She asks questions and makes statements all of which eventually force Catherine to confront some uncomfortable truths about her relationship with Eddie. The suggestion is that Catherine's attachment to Eddie prevents her breaking free from him. Beatrice does not wish to hurt Catherine but she is insistent.

y

A Identify the speaker.

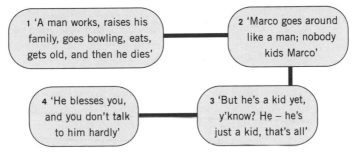

1 'A man works, raises his family, goes bowling, eats, gets old, and then he dies'

2 'Marco goes around like a man; nobody kids Marco'

4 'He blesses you, and you don't talk to him hardly'

3 'But he's a kid yet, y'know? He – he's just a kid, that's all'

Identify the person 'to whom' this comment refers.

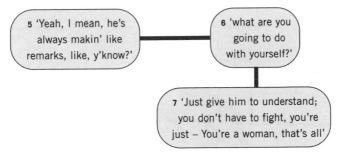

5 'Yeah, I mean, he's always makin' like remarks, like, y'know?'

6 'what are you going to do with yourself?'

7 'Just give him to understand; you don't have to fight, you're just – You're a woman, that's all'

Check your answers on page 62.

B Consider these issues.

a Eddie's obsessive nature.

b Eddie's attitude towards Rodolpho.

c Catherine's attempt to defend Rodolpho.

d How Beatrice is affected by the breakdown of her relationship with Eddie.

e Catherine's reaction to the advice given to her by Beatrice when they are alone.

f The real meaning behind the words 'It means you gotta be your own self more' (p. 43).

g The fear expressed by Catherine at the end of her conversation with Beatrice.

PART THREE

(pp. 45–58)   Alfieri is puzzled when Eddie comes to see him. He tries
to explain to Eddie that no crime has been committed
even though Eddie may think that Rodolpho wants to
marry Catherine in order to make him a legal immigrant.
Eddie then attempts to persuade the lawyer that
Rodolpho is not like an ordinary man because he is too
effeminate. Alfieri tells Eddie that the law would be
interested in Marco and Rodolpho only as illegal
immigrants but Eddie dismisses that idea as indeed Alfieri
Note Alfieri's   knows he will. The lawyer advises him to let Catherine go
function in the   and he angers Eddie when he hints that there may be
play.   more than family love in Eddie's mind. After Eddie's exit
the lawyer meditates on his feeling of doom.

Marco and Rodolpho relate some more details about
their lives in Italy and we see how little Catherine and
Eddie know about their cousins. Marco is happy that
he can send money to his family but he makes it clear
how much he misses his wife and children. Eddie
compounds Marco's misery when he suggests that
Marco's wife might be unfaithful. Rodolpho tells Eddie
that there is a very strict code of morality in his
country. Eddie counters by saying that perhaps

Rodolpho is breaking the unwritten code of America in the cavalier way he has been taking Catherine out without his permission. Eddie repeats his assertion that Rodolpho should be working, not having a good time. Marco supports Eddie.

Look at the conflict between Eddie and Marco. Consider how this conflict intensifies as the play gathers pace.

Catherine and Rodolpho dance. Eddie reflects darkly that Rodolpho's abilities to cook, dance, sing and make dresses do not qualify him for work on the dockyards. He then attempts to show Rodolpho how to box. The encounter ends with Eddie landing a punch which staggers Rodolpho. Catherine is unhappy about this and so is Marco. He challenges Eddie to a chair lifting competition. Eddie accepts but fails. Marco easily lifts the chair above his head and there is a tension between them as Eddie realises that Marco is warning him.

COMMENT   Alfieri now becomes one of the characters (see Literary Terms) in the drama itself.

Eddie passionately states his case. He believes that Alfieri should be capable of proving that Rodolpho is breaking the law. Alfieri points out that Eddie is merely supposing what is inside Rodolpho's mind. Eddie attempts to prove that Rodolpho is not a real man – 'he ain't right' (p. 46). He states that his hair is platinum, he sings in a high voice like a girl, he can cut out dresses and he is laughed at when he goes to work.

Be aware of the unreasonableness shown by Eddie throughout the rest of the play.

These are statements of a desperate man who is blinkered to reason. Eddie refuses to accept Alfieri's logical explanation that the law has not been broken.

The audience now hears Eddie say what is, perhaps, his most significant pronouncement so far:

> 'But I know what they're laughin' at, and when I think of that guy layin' his hands on her I could – I mean it's eatin' me out, Mr Alfieri, because I struggled for that girl. And now he comes in my house and –' (p. 47).

Eddie's frustration is embodied in these lines. He feels a desperation which he does not fully verbalise but it is possible that the audience can sense what he is really saying – that Catherine is rejecting Eddie who is a real man and a man who 'struggled for her' unlike this effeminate boy.

Eddie is quick to dismiss Alfieri's suggestion that the only point of law that can be addressed is that of 'illegal immigration'. He gives the impression that the very idea is against his principles.

Alfieri's main concern is that Eddie is too involved with Catherine. He attempts to tell him tactfully when he explains that Eddie loves Catherine 'too much'.

Eddie voices his desperate feeling of helplessness. Suddenly the audience feels that Eddie may be forcing himself to behave in a manner he may regret.

Notice Alfieri's unsuccessful attempt to save Eddie from himself.

Alfieri feels helpless in the face of Eddie's desperation. He knows that Eddie is about to destroy himself and, perhaps, those near to him.

Beatrice and Catherine create a scene of harmonious domesticity as they talk to the men about life back in Italy. However the undercurrent of Eddie's anger is sensed on every occasion he speaks to Rodolpho.

Eddie controls and then destroys the relaxed mood of the family.

When Marco says that he is unhappy because of his separation from his family Eddie's unpleasant comment about the unfaithfulness of Italian women upsets Marco further. Rodolpho points out that there is a strict code of morality in his country. Eddie is quick to seize the opportunity to turn the conversation to his advantage. He pointedly tells Rodolpho that the American code is no less strict than it is in Italy, and that Rodolpho himself is breaking this code.

Beatrice encourages Catherine's show of independence when the girl asks Rodolpho to dance.

Study Eddie's attempts to show his superiority over Rodolpho.

It now becomes very important to Eddie that he assert himself over Rodolpho. He sneers at the Italian's ability to cook inferring that it is not manly to cook. He follows this with further comments on his ability to sing and make dresses. He is careful, however, not to criticise Rodolpho too openly. Instead he comments on his own shortcomings compared to the skills of Rodolpho.

Eddie tears his newspaper in two thus making the point that he, a real man, could quite easily break Rodolpho if he so wished.

The trial of strength that follows is full of tension and pathos (see Literary Terms). While Eddie 'teaches' Rodolpho to box the tension is shown through the reactions of the others.

- Beatrice, after her initial alarm, sees only what she considers friendly rivalry.
- Catherine is fearful for Rodolpho's safety. She is showing that, if necessary, she will take sides.
- Marco is cautious at first but then decides to react. He sees Eddie's action as hostile and deliberately challenges him to a trial of strength.

This contest is important because it shows that, when it really matters, Marco will always be loyal to Rodolpho and also that he, Marco, will be the stronger if Eddie attempts to show further aggression towards either of the brothers.

TEST YOURSELF (Act I, Part Three)

A Identify the speaker.

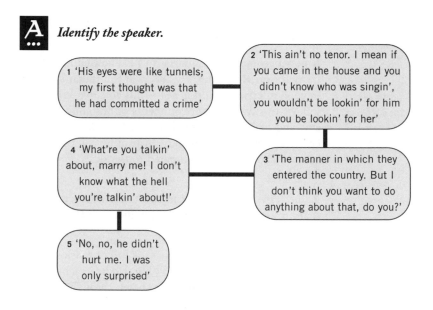

1 'His eyes were like tunnels; my first thought was that he had committed a crime'

2 'This ain't no tenor. I mean if you came in the house and you didn't know who was singin', you wouldn't be lookin' for him you be lookin' for her'

4 'What're you talkin' about, marry me! I don't know what the hell you're talkin' about!'

3 'The manner in which they entered the country. But I don't think you want to do anything about that, do you?'

5 'No, no, he didn't hurt me. I was only surprised'

Identify the person 'to whom' this comment refers.

6 'I knew where he was heading for, I knew where he was going to end'

7 'Ya'can't tell, one a these days somebody's liable to step on his foot or sump'm'

Check your answers on page 62.

B Consider these issues.

a Alfieri's powerlessness to stop the events that are about to happen.

b How Arthur Miller builds the drama towards the climax (see Literary Terms) at the end of the act.

c The pain suffered by Marco because of his separation from his family.

d Eddie's brutality when speaking to Marco.

e Eddie's hostility to the independence shown by Rodolpho.

Y

ACT II

PART ONE

(pp. 59–77)
Alfieri tells the audience that this is the first time that Rodolpho and Catherine have been together in the house. Catherine asks Rodolpho what it would be like if they were married and lived in Italy. He replies that they would be 'crazy' to do so – that they would be going back to poverty. Catherine asks him if he would still marry her even if they went to live in Italy. Rodolpho makes it quite clear that he will not marry Catherine just so that he can become an American citizen. Catherine then tells him of her reluctance to leave Eddie because he has been so good to her. Rodolpho tells her that she must break free of Eddie's influence. Catherine cries, they hold each other and then enter the bedroom.

Observe the total sincerity shown by Rodolpho in his dealings with Catherine.

Eddie returns unexpectedly. Catherine appears from the bedroom followed by Rodolpho. Eddie is devastated and orders Rodolpho to leave. Catherine, instead, makes an effort to go but Eddie grabs her and kisses her. Rodolpho protests and tells him that she is going to be his wife. Eddie asks him what he is going to be and then kisses him. Catherine attacks her uncle who laughs at Rodolpho.

Eddie tells Catherine not to provoke him. He leaves after adding veiled threats to Rodolpho.

Note Alfieri's concern about Eddie, which increases, the feeling that Eddie is about to destroy himself.

Alfieri is very concerned about Eddie and about his general appearance. He discovers from Eddie that Marco has not been informed of the incident between Rodolpho and Eddie. Eddie asks for the lawyer's help but once again Alfieri emphasises that the law has not been broken and therefore Eddie must accept the situation as it is. If he does not, Alfieri insists, then he will be the loser.

Part One (pp. 59–77)

Note how Eddie
betrays the
brothers.

Eddie now phones the Immigration Bureau and tells the officer that he wishes to report two illegal immigrants. He gives the address but refuses to give his name.

He returns home to discover Beatrice on her own. Marco and Rodolpho have moved upstairs to the rented accommodation. Beatrice is obviously very angry with Eddie and tells him that she does not want to hear any more from him about Rodolpho and Catherine. Eddie repeats his assertion that there is something not quite right about the Italian. Beatrice pleads with him to let Catherine go. Eddie tells her that he does not want any more discussion about what happens in his bedroom. Beatrice says that she accepts this.

She now tells Eddie that Catherine and Rodolpho are going to be married next week because of fears that Rodolpho might be arrested. Suddenly Eddie is crying and wants to leave the house. Catherine comes down and tells him that if he wants to be at the wedding it will take place on Saturday. Eddie tries to persuade her to go out and meet other boys but she is determined that the wedding will go ahead.

Observe
Catherine's new
found strength.

Beatrice tells Eddie that Marco and Rodolpho are sharing rooms with two other illegal immigrants upstairs. Eddie is stunned by this news and says that Beatrice should get the men out of the house. He worries that they might have been followed. He also worries about what their families might do to him if the immigrants are arrested.

The conversation is interrupted by the arrival of the Immigration Officers. Immediately it is obvious that Beatrice and Catherine suspect that Eddie is responsible for this betrayal.

The officers find four men upstairs and lead them out of the house. As he leaves, Marco spits in Eddie's face. Eddie threatens to kill Marco, who turns and accuses Eddie of stealing the food from his children. The neighbours turn away from Eddie as he protests his innocence.

COMMENT

Alfieri introduces Act II in a good-humoured manner and ends his introduction with the loaded comment:

'Catherine told me later that this was the first time they had been alone together in the house' (p. 59).

The scene which follows is tender and loving. The audience sees the strength of feeling that Catherine and Rodolpho have for one another.

Study the growth of the relationship between Catherine and Rodolpho.

It is important to Catherine, however, that Rodolpho banishes her doubts, the seeds of which were laid earlier by Eddie. In response to her question Rodolpho answers that he would be 'crazy' if he took her back to Italy as his wife.

He also makes it clear to Catherine, and to the audience, that his intentions are genuine. He realises that the question has already been asked by Eddie and he is infuriated by this.

Rodolpho advises Catherine that she must break away from Eddie but she insists that she is the only person

Part One (pp. 59–77)

who really understands his needs and she does not know why she has to 'make a stranger out of him'.

Rodolpho is very gentle, even sympathetic, but still strongly advises that Eddie must let her go. Catherine responds by showing her helplessness. She wants Rodolpho to make love to her and he leads her gently towards the bedroom.

Arthur Miller shows the audience that the relationship between Catherine and Rodolpho is stronger and more fulfilling than that between Beatrice and Eddie.

When Eddie enters he is drunk and his anger rises as he sees what is happening between Catherine and Rodolpho. His outburst overrides all their protestations and he shows his brutal nature when he kisses first Catherine and then Rodolpho.

The threat uttered by Eddie at the end of their struggle is too powerful to be ignored: 'Don't make me do nuthin', Catherine. Watch your step, submarine. By rights they oughta throw you back in the water. But I got pity for you' (p. 65).

Catherine and Rodolpho are left in no doubt that they will be powerless if Eddie decides to act.

Alfieri recognises the terrible change that has come over Eddie and the emptiness of his spirit. He knows, because of the inevitability of the tragedy (see Literary Terms) that is about to happen that he should do something to prevent it but he feels powerless to do so.

Notice the fact that Alfieri cannot prevent Eddie's destruction.

When Eddie tells Alfieri about the struggle it is significant that he omits to tell him about his kissing Catherine and Rodolpho. Alfieri warns Eddie that he must let nature take its course.

When Eddie does phone the Immigration Bureau he is cautious. He believes that if he does not give his name he will not be discovered.

Eddie refuses his friends' invitation to go bowling mainly because his mind is now completely focused on what has happened and on what is about to happen.

Eddie is furious when he discovers Catherine is upstairs with Marco and Rodolpho. Beatrice tries desperately to make him see that he is becoming irrational.

Look for the changes in Catherine.

Catherine is cold, almost calculating. She will not be diverted. She makes it quite clear to Eddie that she is marrying Rodolpho and that there is no way he can stop that happening. The audience now sees that at this moment in the play Catherine has frozen out all the love she had for Eddie.

Eddie is distraught when he discovers that Lipari's nephew is in the house with Marco and Rodolpho. His betrayal now takes on a new dimension.

The Immigration Officers are direct and uncompromising despite their own Italian connections. As far as they are concerned the law is the law and transcends any patriotic feelings they might have.

Beatrice speaks to Eddie just three times but her words make it clear that any denial of responsibility for this act of betrayal will be useless.

Be aware of the public and private condemnation of Eddie.

Arthur Miller now introduces a series of words and actions which show the audience how completely Eddie has lost the respect of those near to him. The most significant point is made by Marco when he spits in Eddie's face. His accusation, 'That one! I accuse that one!' (p. 77) is heard by the group outside. Lipari turns his back on Eddie as do his friends Louis and Mike.

Finally, we hear Catherine condemn Eddie as she pleads with Marco not to do anything he will regret, 'To hell with Eddie. Nobody is gonna talk to him again if he lives to be a hundred' (p. 78).

A *Identify the speaker.*

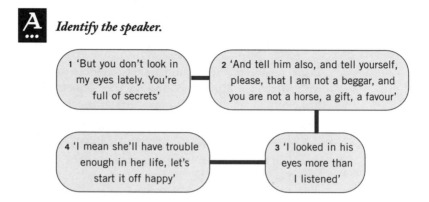

1 'But you don't look in my eyes lately. You're full of secrets'

2 'And tell him also, and tell yourself, please, that I am not a beggar, and you are not a horse, a gift, a favour'

4 'I mean she'll have trouble enough in her life, let's start it off happy'

3 'I looked in his eyes more than I listened'

Identify the person 'to whom' this comment refers.

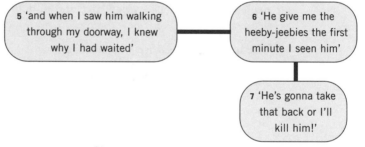

5 'and when I saw him walking through my doorway, I knew why I had waited'

6 'He give me the heeby-jeebies the first minute I seen him'

7 'He's gonna take that back or I'll kill him!'

Check your answers on page 62.

B *Consider these issues.*

a The love Rodolpho has for Catherine.

b Eddie's brutal behaviour when he returns to the home.

c Eddie's concept of manliness.

d Eddie's betrayal of the brothers.

e The reactions of Catherine, Beatrice and Marco to the betrayal.

f Eddie's denial in the face of overwhelming evidence.

g The concepts of justice and law.

PART TWO

(pp. 77–85)

Rodolpho, Marco and Catherine are in the reception room of the prison. Alfieri is waiting for Marco's assurance that he will not attack Eddie. Marco finds it difficult to agree because he feels Eddie should be made to pay for what he has done. Alfieri points out that it is *Study the idea of justice presented by Marco.* only God who delivers ultimate justice. Catherine and Rodolpho urge him to agree because they both want him at their wedding. Alfieri argues that he can, at least, work for six weeks before the trial. Marco finally agrees.

Study the idea of justice presented by Marco.

Beatrice prepares to attend the wedding but Eddie tells her that if she goes she is not to come back to the house. Catherine enters and suddenly attacks Eddie verbally. She tells him that he has no rights any more and when Beatrice explains that she cannot go to the wedding Catherine calls him a rat who bites people as they sleep.

Rodolpho enters. He tells Eddie that Marco is praying in the church before coming for Eddie. Beatrice is *Consider the reasons for Eddie's refusal to leave.* frightened and attempts to persuade Eddie to go away with her. Eddie insists that he wants his name back, his name that Marco took away from him. Rodolpho attempts to take all the blame for what has happened but Eddie merely brushes him aside.

Consider the reasons for Eddie's refusal to leave.

Beatrice, at last, tells Eddie that he cannot have Catherine and he must let her go. This truth shocks Catherine. Eddie is outraged that Beatrice should say this aloud.

Marco enters and Eddie repeats his own name three times. He calls to Marco to give him his name to say that he, Marco, is a liar. Instead, Marco calls him an animal. Eddie lunges for Marco who strikes him and he falls. As Marco raises his foot Eddie draws a knife and

Part Two (pp. 77–85)

lunges at him. Marco turns the knife and stabs Eddie. Catherine protests that she didn't mean any harm. Eddie dies in Beatrice's arms.

Alfieri concludes by saying that it is better to settle for less than the whole truth, but while he believes this, he says he still loves Eddie because he allowed people to see him as he was – completely.

COMMENT

Note Alfieri's role as one who tries to prevent inevitable tragedy.

Alfieri is again involved as the mediator when he attempts to persuade Marco that he must not take revenge. Marco is appealing to a justice that is above and beyond the law. Marco says:

'The law? All the law is not in a book.
...
He degraded my brother. My blood. He robbed my children, he mocks my work. I work to come here, mister!' (p. 79).

Arthur Miller now pushes the drama on relentlessly as the audience sees Beatrice preparing to go to the wedding and Eddie telling her that if she goes she must not come back to him.

The impasse between Eddie and Marco is now impossibly wide as we hear Eddie echo what Marco has said to Alfieri – he expects or says he expects Marco to apologise to him.

Consider the loyalty shown by Beatrice.

Catherine builds on the venom she poured on Eddie previously when she makes it clear that she regards him as 'This rat!' (p. 81). She is clearly upset when Beatrice says that she cannot betray Eddie by going to the wedding. There is a finality to what Beatrice says: 'Now go, go to your wedding, Katie. I'll stay home. Go. God bless you. God bless your children' (p. 81).

Rodolpho's warning to Eddie goes unheeded. Instead Eddie turns on the three of them to demand that his respect be returned to him. And then at last, because he will not listen to reason, Beatrice says it openly: 'You want somethin' else, Eddie, and you can never have her!' (p. 83).

Catherine and Eddie are horrified but Beatrice follows on: 'The truth is not as bad as blood, Eddie. I'm tellin' you the truth – tell her good-bye for ever'.

Look at Eddie's reactions to the statement by Beatrice. Perhaps he wants the confrontation to end in death.

Eddie will not accept this accusation and turns instead to face the challenge of Marco. This he can deal with and, indeed, will do so.

He has convinced himself that he is justified in asking for his self-respect.

If nothing else, Eddie has a tremendous capacity for self-delusion. His speech of self-justification is delivered with his family, friends and neighbours as audience. He calls on Marco to apologise to him for taking away his name. He lists the wrongs he has endured and also the hospitality he has freely given. Very deliberately Eddie forces the issue until he has created a confrontation from which Marco cannot withdraw.

Part Two (pp. 77–85)

Marco strikes Eddie, Eddie draws a knife and Marco turns the knife on Eddie. Eddie's final line indicates that he believes he has been wronged by Catherine and, therefore, by Rodolpho, Marco and even Beatrice. To the end he shows his capacity for self-delusion.

Alfieri closes the play with a speech to the audience which tells us that he cannot help but be impressed by a man who did not compromise, 'who allowed himself to be wholly known' (p. 85).

Consider the thought that 'it is better to settle for half.'

He knows that it is better to 'settle for half' but he finds it necessary to convince himself.

His final line shows the contradictory nature of his feelings for Eddie: 'And so I mourn for him with a certain … alarm' (p. 85).

A   *Identify the speaker.*

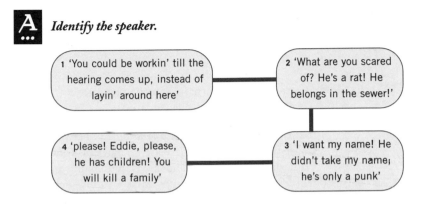

1 'You could be workin' till the hearing comes up, instead of layin' around here'

2 'What are you scared of? He's a rat! He belongs in the sewer!'

4 'please! Eddie, please, he has children! You will kill a family'

3 'I want my name! He didn't take my name; he's only a punk'

Identify the person 'to whom' this comment refers.

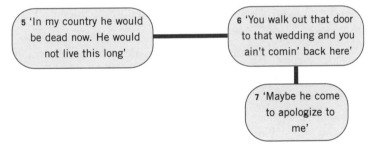

5 'In my country he would be dead now. He would not live this long'

6 'You walk out that door to that wedding and you ain't comin' back here'

7 'Maybe he come to apologize to me'

Check your answers on page 62.

B   *Consider these issues.*

a Marco's intent to kill Eddie.

b Justice as being outside the law.

c Eddie's efforts to re-establish control in his house.

d Catherine's disgust at Eddie's behaviour.

e Rodolpho's attempt to prevent bloodshed.

f The shift in Eddie's hostility from Rodolpho to Marco.

g Beatrice's efforts to force Eddie to accept his unnatural love for Catherine.

h Eddie's refusal to accept his wife's accusation.

PART THREE

COMMENTARY

THEMES

THE RELATIONSHIP BETWEEN EDDIE AND CATHERINE

At the beginning of the play we are immediately aware that there is a lively, intimate relationship between Catherine and Eddie. There are no barriers, as far as Catherine is concerned, and she is quite happy to show herself and her clothes to her uncle. Eddie is delighted at her beauty but because of this beauty he fears what other men will see. She will no longer be his girl – she will belong to the world – and the men – outside. Catherine is unhappy when Eddie does not fully accept the changes in her.

Eddie will not allow Catherine her freedom.

Catherine is further unsettled when Eddie will not accept that Catherine should take a job. His possessiveness is now more obvious than it was at the beginning. If Catherine goes out into the world of work she will consort with the male population every day. This unsettles Eddie. Beatrice comments about Eddie's relationship with Catherine on a number of occasions throughout the play. When Catherine leaves the room at the beginning Beatrice tries to make Eddie see that he is smothering Catherine and stifling the independence to which Catherine is entitled.

Study Eddie's reaction to Rodolpho's character.

When the cousins arrive Eddie is quickly aware of the attraction Rodolpho has for Catherine and from this moment onwards Eddie attempts to place a barrier between them.

Eddie feels out of his depth and cannot compete with the new worlds and experiences that Rodolpho is introducing to Catherine. This creates further conflict between the two men and also between Eddie and

Catherine. Eddie can now see that she is no longer his possession because she is very attracted to this new life and her new exciting boyfriend. The audience can see that when Eddie makes a derogatory comment about Rodolpho he does so out of anger and frustration and that his attempts to keep Catherine for himself are unsuccessful.

There is a significant moment in Act I when Eddie asks Catherine if she likes Rodolpho. Her simple answer, 'Yeah I like him', contains a rejection of her ties with Eddie and he is fully aware of this.

Study all the comments made by Eddie when he speaks about Rodolpho.

In a desperate attempt to force her to break her connection with Rodolpho, Eddie accuses Rodolpho of using Catherine to gain legal entry into the United States. This he hopes will force her to return to her dependence on him. However, Eddie's attempt to denigrate the Italian does not succeed and instead Catherine tells Eddie that Rodolpho's love for her is genuine. Eddie cannot accept what she says and immediately goes to Beatrice for support. Beatrice has no sympathy for him. Instead she accuses Eddie of not leaving Catherine alone and she is obviously losing patience with Eddie.

Beatrice tries hard to tell Eddie that he must let Catherine go, that he must allow her freedom to have her relationship with Rodolpho. It is not until the end of the play that Beatrice says, quite specifically, that Eddie cannot have the relationship he wants with Catherine. But Eddie will not accept what she says – at least outwardly. However, the audience has no doubt that he knows what Beatrice has said is true. This is why he reacts in such an explosive way – as if to shut out the truth. Indeed, at this time the challenge from Marco is welcomed by Eddie as a way to destroy his awareness of the truth. Beatrice also confronts Catherine with the truth about her relationship with Eddie. She very gently attempts to persuade Catherine that she must break free. Catherine, however, is aware that she will 'kick him in the face' if she rejects Eddie totally. It may be, of course, that she does not wish to leave the security that her relationship with Eddie gives her.

Consider Eddie's reactions to Alfieri's comments about the relationship.

Like Beatrice, Alfieri is aware of the dangerous nature of the relationship. He also warns Eddie that he must not feel as he does for Catherine. Tactfully he tells him that the relationship has a darker side that must not be allowed to blossom. Eddie reacts angrily and refuses to accept that the relationship is anything other than that of an ordinary relationship between uncle and niece. Every statement made by Alfieri makes it clear that the relationship must end now or it will, eventually, have tragic consequences.

In the end, of course, Catherine's hostile attack on Eddie is a statement that she has now finally broken free from him. The break in the relationship is now complete.

MANLINESS

Notice Eddie's rejection of Rodolpho. He sees Rodolpho as less than a 'real man'.

Eddie has a very narrow view of what he considers manliness. He may never say it but he feels that manliness consists of knowing one's boundaries and protecting one's territory, territory in which other men are regarded as hostile intruders if they attempt to enter.

Rodolpho's behaviour unsettles Eddie. He does not regard him as a real man as Rodolpho cooks, sings, makes dresses and has platinum hair. He calls him 'Paper Doll', 'canary' and 'a weird'. Beatrice attempts to show him how unreasonable he is being when she suggests that he is jealous of Rodolpho. Eddie rejects this idea.

Beatrice is warm and sensitive. She welcomes the cousins openly. Eddie, however, keeps his distance. He does not regard it as manly to show his emotions in this open way. His comments and questions have usually got an edge to them that make the other characters (see Literary Terms) feel uncomfortable or indeed threatened.

Eddie's own masculinity is called into question when Beatrice asks him 'When am I gonna be a wife again, Eddie?' Later in the play, when he is attempting to regain control in his own home he tells Beatrice that she must never ask questions like this again.

Generally speaking Eddie is a simple man who feels uncomfortable when the boundaries of his manliness are threatened. When he is confused he refuses to accept anything other than his own uncomplicated measure of masculinity.

JUSTICE AND THE LAW

Consider the idea that total justice is not possible to dispense.

Alfieri, as a lawyer, is aware that the law, despite its limitations, must be upheld. However, he is also aware of the inability of the law to dispense total justice. He feels powerless to intervene when a character (see Literary Terms) in the play decides to find justice in his own way – outside the law.

Eddie Carbone is a man who does not understand the reasons for the limitations of the law. Early in the play he asks Beatrice to tell Catherine the story of Vinny Bolzano. In Eddie's eyes and in the eyes of the community Vinny was guilty of injustice and his family ensured that justice was done when he was punished and shunned by the neighbourhood.

There is a feeling that if people always abide by the law then they will have to 'settle for half'. Alfieri seems to be saying that the law is often incapable of satisfying everybody.

Eddie tries to force Alfieri to give him his kind of justice. He believes (or says that he believes) that Rodolpho is going to marry Catherine in order to make him a legal immigrant. He feels that this is unjust and that the law should be capable of making a case against Rodolpho. Alfieri is very rational and unemotional as he informs Eddie that no law has been broken.

The real injustice as far as Eddie is concerned is that Rodolpho, who, according to Eddie, is an effeminate 'weird guy', is taking Catherine for his own and away from Eddie who is, in his own opinion, all that a man should be.

Look at Alfieri's attempt to persuade Eddie that natural justice is very important.

Alfieri warns Eddie that if he betrays the brothers he will be breaching the code of his people and that they will turn against him. Here Alfieri is placing the law against natural justice – he is emphasising that it would be unjust to betray the Italians even if Eddie is actually upholding the law by reporting them.

In the final section of the play Marco demands justice and, as he does so, he echoes the sentiments spoken earlier by Eddie. He says 'The law? All the law is not in the book' (p. 79). He talks about honour and he talks about blood and about degradation all of which matter to Marco when he speaks of justice. Again, Alfieri cautions against stepping outside the law.

Throughout the play there is an emphasis on justice, but as Alfieri tells us there is a price to pay for total justice – a price that most people, most of the time, are not prepared to pay. This is why the majority feel that 'it is better to settle for half'.

STRUCTURE

Notice the
importance of
Alfieri's role in the
structure of the
play.

A View from the Bridge is a well-structured play with an uncomplicated shape. The play is in two acts but within these acts there are a number of easily defined divisions which are controlled by the lawyer, Alfieri. Alfieri is essential to the structure (see Literary Terms) of the play. He opens and closes the play and at other times we see him as Arthur Miller's mouthpiece moving the action quickly onwards.

All the action revolves around Eddie Carbone. His character (see Literary Terms) controls the drama. When he is calm and friendly, the atmosphere (see Literary Terms) is likewise. When he is tense and hostile the atmosphere is uncomfortable. There are a number of flashpoints in the two acts which echo one another. The controlled hostility at the end of Act I (when Eddie shows Rodolpho how to box and Marco indirectly challenges Eddie) is developed into unpleasant hostility at the beginning of Act II when Eddie kisses Catherine and Rodolpho. The final explosive violence at the end of the drama is justified when we consider what has gone before.

The themes of the play, incest, justice, manliness (see Themes) are woven into the action and are always part of the fabric of the drama. Arthur Miller moves the action and the themes simply and forcefully through the play until he reaches the final tragic scene.

EDDIE

Forceful
Obsessive
Warm
Protective
Irrational
Self-interested

Eddie is the main character (see Literary Terms) in the play and every significant act in the drama is connected to him. He is forceful, energetic and obsessive. He is capable of self-delusion on a grand scale. He is also, however, a character who can show warmth and some generosity.

He is protective towards Catherine at the beginning of the play and he does not wish her to expose herself to the attentions of the men of the neighbourhood. He comments on her clothes and the way she looks. His interest in Catherine soon becomes obsessive and is obviously unnatural. He lays down rules for Catherine to live by and he finds it impossible to accept that she should have a life of her own apart from her relationship with him.

Eddie is a man who has few interests outside the family and, in the end, no interests, apart from himself and his relationship with Catherine.

Eddie's changes of mood can be quite sharp. Even when joking about the sacrifices he has to make for the coming of Beatrice's cousins there is an unpleasant edge to his comments. It is difficult for any of the characters to be completely at ease with Eddie. There are few moments in the play when he is not in conflict. Much of their time is spent in attempting to placate him.

Before the cousins arrive Eddie creates the impression that he is the authority in his own household. He lays down the rules and it is to him that Beatrice and Catherine must refer if they wish to deviate from the routine that has been established. When the play opens we sense an air of unease because Catherine and Beatrice are unsure of what Eddie's reaction will be when he is told about Catherine's job.

Eddie's reaction to Rodolpho demonstrates how emotionally unstable and irrational he is. His jealousy of the young man drives him to accuse him of being homosexual, effeminate and he also accuses him that he is only interested in Catherine because she could be his passport to achieving full American citizenship.

Self-interest is one of Eddie's great motivating factors. He is deeply aware of the horrific nature of betraying an immigrant to the authorities and yet, when his own comfortable relationship with Catherine is threatened, he is quite prepared to break this code of honour. Later, he will not accept the truth when Marco accuses him of betrayal and, instead, tries to plead for support against Marco's 'lies'.

In the end Eddie realises that his honourable 'name' is at stake. He has betrayed his name and he has lost the respect of all those who know him and therefore he has no option but to face Marco in mortal combat. Perhaps, in the end, he gains some dignity in the way he dies. In any case, as Alfieri says, Eddie 'allowed himself to be wholly known'.

BEATRICE

Beatrice is loving and caring. She is capable of taking an overview of the situations as they occur. She is often the mediator when Eddie's aggressiveness creates hostile situations. She can, however, be quite assertive when she feels the occasion demands. It is she who attempts to warn Eddie that his relationship with Catherine is not within acceptable bounds. Catherine is also warned by Beatrice that she is contributing to Eddie's infatuation. Beatrice feels that Eddie does not behave as a husband should and she indicates that he has not made love to her for some time. She knows her rights as a wife and she is not prepared to let Eddie

Loving
Caring
Mediator
Assertive
Represents
reason and
sanity

ignore these rights especially as it seems that his infatuation with Catherine is the root cause.

Beatrice is the thread of reason that runs throughout the play. She is always able to rise above any situation created by Eddie and she is always prepared to do whatever is necessary to recreate sanity in their lives even to the extent of refusing to go to Catherine's wedding because Eddie does not want her to. She is the one who is always attempting to pull Eddie back from the edge of darkness. And when he does slip over the edge she is the one who is there to comfort him.

CATHERINE

Lively
Innocent
Open
Initially
influenced by
Eddie
Gains
independence

Catherine is a lively young women who is eager to experience the world. She is innocent and open, always ready to love and be loved. However, she has no real experience until Rodolpho enters her life. Until now her security has been bound to her relationship with Eddie and Beatrice. She is genuinely unaware that there is anything improper in her relationship with Eddie and is horrified when Beatrice suggests that there might be more to the bond than she realises.

She is heavily influenced by Eddie and, for this reason, she is doubtful about Rodolpho's motives in marrying her. She quickly accepts his assurances, however, and this is the moment when she abandons herself to him. She now accepts her love for Rodolpho without restraint. She takes sides against Eddie and is quite vehement in her condemnation of his actions when he betrays Rodolpho and Marco. This is the point in the play where she shows a strength of character that has not been in evidence before. However, any strength this might have given her evaporates in the final moments of the play when she murmurs her heartfelt regret for her part in Eddie's tragic end.

y

Marco

Responsible

Strong sense of justice

Focused

Strong

When he enters, Marco is seen as the stronger of the two brothers. He is only too well aware of his obligations to Eddie and this is why he is happy to suggest to Rodolpho that his brother should not behave in a manner that will upset Eddie. His strong sense of responsibility to his wife and family is obvious and is, therefore, the only reason he has come to America. He gives the impression that he thinks before he acts.

However, he has a strong sense of right and wrong and an even stronger sense of justice. When he sees Eddie hitting his brother he is quick to show Eddie that he, the stronger man, will be there to defend Rodolpho if necessary. When his mind is made up he is totally focused – he employs tunnel vision.

Marco's intention to punish Eddie is not a selfish one, he feels that it is his duty to do so. If the law will not help him he will take the law into his own hands. His sense of morality is very clear. We are not absolutely certain that Marco would have killed Eddie if Eddie had not pulled a knife on him but, having said that, Arthur Miller does not allow Marco to express any sorrow or regret for the death of Eddie. Marco is the character (see Literary Terms) about whom Arthur Miller tells us least. He is the antagonist (see Literary Terms) in the play and the Sicilian avenging angel that Alfieri hints at in his comment to the audience.

Rodolpho

Rodolpho makes an immediate impact when he enters. Catherine and Beatrice find him an attractive young man and his lively sense of humour endears him to the audience. He is delighted to be in America as his very

Attractive
Humorous
Intelligent
Talented
Thoughtful
Sensitive

first line makes clear. His command of the language is impressive even though Arthur Miller makes it obvious that English is not his first language. His use of words and images show a lightness of touch that betrays an intelligent mind at work. He is a man of many talents – many of which are sneered at by Eddie. He can cook, he can sing and he can make clothes. Eddie's hostility upsets him mainly because he cannot understand why Eddie should dislike him.

Rodolpho, more than any other character (see Literary Terms), has a love of life in all its forms and he has a tendency to influence other characters with his ebullience. Catherine falls in love with him very quickly and Rodolpho's love for her is genuine and powerful. This is nowhere more evident than at the beginning of Act II when the audience hears his reasons for staying in America with Catherine as his bride.

It is interesting to note the change in roles between Rodolpho and Marco as the play progresses. At first Marco is seen as the strong one, the leader, the 'reasonable' brother. However, at the end of the play we see Rodolpho as the thoughtful, sensitive young man who has the vision to see what terrible consequences will result from the battle of wills between Marco and Eddie. He attempts to persuade Marco not to harm Eddie, he apologises to Eddie for his behaviour and finally tries to warn Eddie that Marco is in no mood to capitulate or compromise. All this shows the audience that Rodolpho is a sensitive, intelligent character who feels a sense of responsibility for those close to him.

ALFIERI

Alfieri is a narrator, commentator and sometimes a character in the play itself. He can sense the terrible

Narrator
Commentator
Oversees action
Objective

Sympathetic

events that are about to happen but is powerless to prevent them (see chorus in Literary Terms). He dispenses information and advice and, most emphatically, explains the law and its boundaries. It is he who attempts to place the events of the drama in context and explain to the audience that conflicts such as those related in the play occur throughout Italian and Sicilian history.

Alfieri talks about 'settling for half' and about liking that better because, quite often, the search for absolute justice results in unacceptable consequences. He realises that the law is limited and cannot deal with every human problem fully. He explains the boundaries to both Marco and Eddie but, even though in his heart he knows they will ignore what he has said to them, he cannot take further action to prevent the conflict.

Arthur Miller has not drawn Alfieri as a full 'flesh and blood' character even though there are times when we feel sympathy for his predicament. Alfieri's role is to oversee the action and remain objective throughout. The audience can see, at the end of the play, that Alfieri does have sympathy for Eddie and even some admiration for him because he was a man 'who allowed himself to be wholly known'. And there, finally, we have Alfieri's most important role. He offers the audience universal concepts to think about as they leave the theatre.

LANGUAGE & STYLE

Note the suitability of the language used by each character.

There are a variety of language forms in *A View from the Bridge*. The audience hears the educated, controlled language of Alfieri, the intelligent attractive conversation of Rodolpho, the heavy serious tones of Marco and then the lively, uneducated speech of Eddie, Catherine and Beatrice.

Alfieri: thoughtful

Eddie, Catherine and Beatrice: simple

The language of Alfieri is meditative and helps the audience to think about the issues which Arthur Miller feels are important. He is easy to listen to and can at times show a wry sense of humour. He is Arthur Miller's spokesman and, as such, is usually removed from the action. Eddie, Catherine and Beatrice speak in short, uncomplicated sentences. Their language gives the impression that quite often the characters (see Literary Terms) speak without thinking and say far less than they really mean. There may be two reasons for this – they may not possess the language to express their ideas or they may not wish to express their innermost thoughts.

Rodolpho: lively, witty

Rodolpho's speech is obviously that of someone who is talking in his second language but his intelligent, sensitive nature shines through the words he uses. He speaks in an attractive, lively way and has the ability to entertain an audience. Catherine and Beatrice are immediately entranced by the descriptions of his home town.

Marco: serious, passionate

Marco's conversation tells the audience that he is a serious man who takes his responsibilities very seriously. His language tells of his serious nature and his intense sense of his responsibilities. At the end of the play he speaks to Eddie a mere five times but each time is full of passion and venom, a passion and venom born of injustice and frustration.

Arthur Miller's genius lies in his ability to write dialogue (see Literary Terms) which is so varied and yet is part of the complete tapestry of the play.

Y

PART FOUR

Study Skills

How to use quotations

One of the secrets of success in writing essays is the way you use quotations. There are five basic principles:

- Put inverted commas at the beginning and end of the quotation
- Write the quotation exactly as it appears in the orginal
- Do not use a quotation that repeats what you have just written
- Use the quotation so that it fits into your sentence
- Keep the quotation as short as possible

Quotations should be used to develop the line of thought in your essays.

Your comment should not duplicate what is in your quotation. For example:

> Eddie Carbone tells Catherine that she must not trust anybody, 'I only ask you one thing – don't trust nobody'.

Far more effective is to write:

> Eddie Carbone tells Catherine to 'trust nobody'.

Always lay out the lines as they appear in the text. Foe example:

> Alfieri is worried about Eddie:
> 'His eyes were like tunnels; my first thought was that he had committed a crime.'

However, the most sophisticated way of using the writer's words is to embed them into your sentence:

> Alfieri feels that compromise is better and that 'now we settle for half'.

When you use quotations in this way, you are demonstrating the ability to use text as evidence to support your ideas – not simply including words from the original to prove you have read it.

Everyone writes differently. Work through the suggestions given here and adapt the advice to suit your own style and interests. This will improve your essay-writing skills and allow your personal voice to emerge.

The following points indicate in ascending order the skills of essay writing:

- Picking out one or two facts about the story and adding the odd detail
- Writing about the text by retelling the story
- Retelling the story and adding a quotation here and there
- Organising an answer which explains what is happening in the text and giving quotations to support what you write

....

- Writing in such a way as to show that you have thought about the intentions of the writer of the text and that you understand the techniques used
- Writing at some length, giving your viewpoint on the text and commenting by picking out details to support your views
- Looking at the text as a work of art, demonstrating clear critical judgement and explaining to the reader of your essay how the enjoyment of the text is assisted by literary devices, linguistic effects and psychological insights; showing how the text relates to the time when it was written

The dotted line above represents the division between lower and higher level grades. Higher-level performance begins when you start to consider your response as a reader of the text. The highest level is reached when you offer an enthusiastic personal response and show how this piece of literature is a product of its time.

Coursework
Essay

Set aside an hour or so at the start of your work to plan what you have to do.

- List all the points you feel are needed to cover the task. Collect page references of information and quotations that will support what you have to say. A helpful tool is the highlighter pen: this saves painstaking copying and enables you to target precisely what you want to use.
- Focus on what you consider to be the main points of the essay. Try to sum up your argument in a single sentence, which could be the closing sentence of your essay. Depending on the essay title, it could be a statement about a character: Marco's decision to punish Eddie is not a selfish one, he feels that it is his duty to do so; an opinion about language: The language used by Beatrice, Catherine and Eddie is incisive and colloquial (see Literary Terms); or a judgement on a theme: One of the main themes in *A View from the Bridge* is justice because Eddie and Marco search for their own type of justice in different ways.
- Make a short essay plan. Use the first paragraph to introduce the argument you wish to make. In the following paragraphs develop this argument with details, examples and other possible points of view. Sum up your argument in the last paragraph. Check you have answered the question.
- Write the essay, remembering all the time the central point you are making.
- On completion, go back over what you have written to eliminate careless errors and improve expression. Read it aloud to yourself, or, if you are feeling more confident, to a relative or friend.

If you can, try to type your essay, using a word processor. This will allow you to correct and improve your writing without spoiling its appearance.

Examination
Essay

The essay written in an examination often carries more marks than the coursework essay even though it is written under considerable time pressure.

In the revision period build up notes on various aspects of the text you are using. Fortunately, in acquiring this set of York Notes on *A View from the Bridge,* you have made a prudent beginning! York Notes are set out to give you vital information and help you to construct your personal overview of the text.

Make notes with appropriate quotations about the key issues of the set text. Go into the examination knowing your text and having a clear set of opinions about it.

In most English Literature examinations, you can take in copies of your set books. This is an enormous advantage although it may lull you into a false sense of security. Beware! There is simply not enough time in an examination to read the book from scratch.

In the
Examination

- Read the question paper carefully and remind yourself what you have to do.
- Look at the questions on your set texts to select the one that most interests you and mentally work out the points you wish to stress.
- Remind yourself of the time available and how you are going to use it.
- Briefly map out a short plan in note form that will keep your writing on track and illustrate the key argument you want to make.
- Then set about writing it.
- When you have finished, check through to eliminate errors.

To summarise,
these are the
keys to success:

- **Know the text**
- **Have a clear understanding of and opinions on the storyline, characters, setting, themes and writer's concerns**
- **Select the right material**
- **Plan and write a clear response, continually bearing the question in mind**

A typical essay question on *A View from the Bridge* is followed by a sample essay plan in note form. This does not present the only answer to the question, merely one answer. Do not be afraid to include your own ideas and leave out some of the ones in this sample! Remember that quotations are essential to prove and illustrate the points you make.

Explore the way Arthur Miller writes about justice in *A View from the Bridge*. Write about the characters' (see Literary Terms) search for justice and the feeling that the law is sometimes inadequate.

Introduction
- Alfieri's thoughts about justice and the law
- Law often inadequate
- Justice not the same for the different characters

Part 1
- The characters' attitude to the law
- No compunction about breaking immigration law or, indeed, other laws
- Betrayal is injustice – Vinny Bolzano
- Irony of Eddie's horror at Vinny's betrayal
- Family meted out their own justice

Part 2
- Eddie's pursuit of justice
- Feels Rodolpho had broken the 'code'
- Alfieri explains the law
- Eddie's frustration that the law cannot give him 'justice'

Part 3
- Eddie's blindness to the injustice he is causing to others
- Not treating Beatrice as a loving husband should
- His obsessive nature smothers Catherine
- His betrayal of the brothers linked to his earlier attitude to Vinny Bolzano

Part 4
- Marco's demands for justice
- Is he more justified than Eddie in demanding vengeance/justice?

- Marco's conversation with Alfieri – compare it with the one Eddie had previously had with the lawyer

Part 5
- Consider Rodolpho's attitude
- Examine his involvement with Eddie and Marco towards end of play
- Is he the one who is prepared to settle for Alfieri's 'half'?

Part 6
- The climax of the play and the terrible consequences of two characters search for justice
- Look at those who lose
- Does anybody win?

Conclusion
- General comment on Arthur Miller's treatment of law and justice

FURTHER QUESTIONS

The following questions require a knowledge of the whole play. You should make a plan like the one on the previous pages before attempting any of the essays.

1 Compare and contrast the characters of Eddie and Marco.

2 Examine the ideas of manliness, hostility and aggression as they are portrayed in the play. How are these ideas connected?

3 Discuss the relationship between Eddie and Beatrice. Do you feel that Eddie's feelings for Catherine interfere with this relationship in any way?

4 What is Alfieri's function in the play?

5 Compare the characters of Marco and Rodolpho.

6 Why does Alfieri say that people should 'settle for half'? Is he right to say this?

7 Write about the relationship between Catherine and Rodolpho. Why does Catherine find Rodolpho attractive?

8 Discuss the theme of betrayal in *A View from the Bridge*.

PART FIVE

CULTURAL CONNECTIONS

BROADER PERSPECTIVES

Arthur Miller's plays have been produced and presented all over the world and have been received to wide critical acclaim. Whenever possible the student should attempt to see the plays in live performance. If this is not possible there are a number of filmed versions of the plays especially *All My Sons*, *Death of a Salesman*, *A View from the Bridge* and *The Crucible*. There is a film version of *The Crucible* that was released in 1997. However, at the present time, these films are not available on video. There are also a number of audio productions which are very useful for home and classroom use.

Henrik Ibsen has always been a powerful influence on Arthur Miller, especially when considering the responsibilities of the public and private individuals. *An Enemy of the People* (Viking, 1951) is readily accessible to the young reader and well worth reading.

Arthur Miller's autobiography (see Literary Terms) *Time Bends* (Methuen, 1987) should be read for the insight it gives into the origin of many of the plays and for his motivation for writing them.

The play *The Caucasian Chalk Circle* (Penguin, 1949) by Bertolt Brecht should be read if only for an examination of the function of 'The Singer' who, like Alfieri, is a narrator and commentator – one of whose functions is to offer ideas to the audience to set them thinking!

It is also worth mentioning *Arthur Miller* (Macmillan, 1982) by Neil Carson which is an excellent introduction to the works of Arthur Miller.

anecdote anecdotes are narratives of small incidents or events, told for the purpose of entertainment, mirth, malice, or to reveal character. In *A View from the Bridge*, Rodolpho tells a number of anecdotes but the most significant story is told by Beatrice when she talks about Vinny Bolzano

antagonist the chief opponent of the hero or protagonist in a story; especially used of drama. Thus Marco is the antagonist in *A View from the Bridge*

atmosphere a common term for the mood – moral, sensational, emotional and intellectual – which dominates a piece of writing

autobiography the story of a person's life written by that person. Arthur Miller's autobiography is called *Time Bends* and provides valuable background material for the study of *A View from the Bridge*

character characters are the invented, imaginary persons in a dramatic work which are given human qualities and behaviour

chorus in the tragedies of the ancient Greek playwright Aeschylus the chorus is a group of characters who represent ordinary people in their attitudes to the action which they witness as bystanders and on which they comment. Alfieri describes the situation of the play as it occurs and often reacts to the action. Like the chorus of the Greek Theatre he is powerless to affect events

climax any point of great intensity in a literary work; in a narrative the culminating moment of the action. In *A View from the Bridge* the climax is discovered when Marco turns the knife on Eddie and kills him

colloquialism the use of the kinds of expression and grammar associated with ordinary, everyday speech rather than formal language. The speech of Catherine, Eddie and Beatrice is regarded as colloquial

dialogue the speech and conversation between characters in any kind of literary work

full-length prose a play that is written in plain speech e.g. the final version of *A View from the Bridge*

genre the term for a kind of literature. The three major genres of literature are poetry, drama and the novel (prose); these kinds may be subdivided into many other genres such as narrative verse, tragedy, comedy, short story and so on

melodrama the most common critical use of the word 'melodrama' or 'melodramatic' is to characterise any kind of writing which relies on sensational happenings, violent action and improbable events. Some critics see *A View from the Bridge* as melodramatic because of its violent ending

monologue a single person speaking with or without an audience is uttering a monologue. Alfieri's speeches to the audience are monologues

pathos moments in works of art which evoke strong feelings of pity and sorrow are said to have this quality

protagonist in Greek drama the principal character and actor. Now used almost synonymously with 'hero' to refer to the leading character in a play. Eddie is the protagonist in *A View from the Bridge* though we might argue about the term 'hero' when referring to him

structure the overall principle of organisation in a work of literature

style the characteristic manner in which a writer expresses him – or herself, or the particular manner of an individual literary work

tragedy possibly the most easily recognised genre in literature and certainly one of the most discussed. Basically a tragedy traces the career and downfall of an individual and shows in this downfall both the capacities and the limitations of human life. The protagonist may be superhuman, a monarch or, in the modern age, an ordinary person. *A View from the Bridge* is regarded as a tragedy by some critics but some also regard it as a melodrama

verse play a play that is written in the poetic form usually in blank verse (i.e. it does not rhyme but it has rhythm) e.g. the original version of *A View from the Bridge*

TEST ANSWERS

TEST YOURSELF (Act I: Part One)

A
1 Alfieri
••• 2 Catherine
3 Beatrice
4 Catherine
5 Rodolpho
6 Marco
7 Catherine

TEST YOURSELF (Act I: Part Two)

A
1 Alfieri
••• 2 Eddie
3 Eddie
4 Catherine
5 Rodolpho
6 Catherine
7 Eddie

TEST YOURSELF (Act I: Part Three)

A
1 Alfieri
••• 2 Eddie
3 Alfieri

4 Eddie
5 Rodolpho
6 Eddie
7 Rodolpho

TEST YOURSELF (Act II: Part One)

A
1 Rodolpho
••• 2 Rodolpho
3 Alfieri
4 Beatrice
5 Eddie
6 Rodolpho
7 Marco

TEST YOURSELF (Act II: Part Two)

A
1 Catherine
••• 2 Catherine
3 Eddie
4 Rodolpho
5 Eddie
6 Beatrice
7 Marco

GCSE and equivalent levels (£3.50 each)

Harold Brighouse
Hobson's Choice

Charles Dickens
Great Expectations

Charles Dickens
Hard Times

George Eliot
Silas Marner

William Golding
Lord of the Flies

Thomas Hardy
The Mayor of Casterbridge

Susan Hill
I'm the King of the Castle

Barry Hines
A Kestrel for a Knave

Harper Lee
To Kill a Mockingbird

Arthur Miller
A View from the Bridge

Arthur Miller
The Crucible

George Orwell
Animal Farm

J.B. Priestley
An Inspector Calls

J.D. Salinger
The Catcher in the Rye

William Shakespeare
Macbeth

William Shakespeare
The Merchant of Venice

William Shakespeare
Romeo and Juliet

William Shakespeare
Twelfth Night

George Bernard Shaw
Pygmalion

John Steinbeck
Of Mice and Men

Mildred D. Taylor
Roll of Thunder, Hear My Cry

James Watson
Talking in Whispers

A Choice of Poets

Nineteenth Century Short Stories

Poetry of the First World War

Advanced level (£3.99 each)

Margaret Atwood
The Handmaid's Tale

Jane Austen
Emma

Jane Austen
Pride and Prejudice

William Blake
Songs of Innocence and of Experience

Charlotte Brontë
Jane Eyre

Emily Brontë
Wuthering Heights

Geoffrey Chaucer
The Wife of Bath's Prologue and Tale

Joseph Conrad
Heart of Darkness

Charles Dickens
Great Expectations

F. Scott Fitzgerald
The Great Gatsby

Thomas Hardy
Tess of the d'Urbervilles

Seamus Heaney
Selected Poems

James Joyce
Dubliners

Arthur Miller
Death of a Salesman

William Shakespeare
Antony and Cleopatra

William Shakespeare
Hamlet

William Shakespeare
King Lear

William Shakespeare
The Merchant of Venice

William Shakespeare
Much Ado About Nothing

William Shakespeare
Othello

William Shakespeare
Romeo and Juliet

William Shakespeare
The Tempest

Mary Shelley
Frankenstein

Alice Walker
The Color Purple

Tennessee Williams
A Streetcar Named Desire

John Webster
The Duchess of Malfi